MEADOW OAKS SCHOOL

Birthday Book Club

Title: ___THE FARM___

Given by: ___MATTHEW BAILEY___

Grade: ___2___ Date: ___APRIL 4, 1998___

DATE DUE

AF.J.D		
3/1/99		
A7		
3-14-07		

...dow Oaks School
...56 Mulholland
...asas, Calif. 91302

The Farm

by Gail Saunders-Smith

Content Consultant:
Leesa Christensen, Education Director
National Farmers Union

Pebble Books
an imprint of Capstone Press

Pebble Books

Pebble Books are published by Capstone Press
818 North Willow Street, Mankato, Minnesota 56001
http://www.capstone-press.com

Library of Congress Cataloging-in-Publication Data
Saunders-Smith, Gail.
    The farm/by Gail Saunders-Smith
    p. cm.
    Includes bibliographical references (p.23) and index.
    Summary: Simple text and photographs depict places on the farm and what farmers do there.
    ISBN 1-56065-774-X
    1. Farms--Juvenile literature. 2. Agriculture--Juvenile literature. [1. Farms. 2. Farm life.
3. Agriculture.] I. Title.
    S519.S23 1998
    630--dc21   98-5044
                                           CIP
                                          AC

Note to Parents and Teachers

This book serves as a visual field trip to a farm, illustrating and describing the various kinds of crops and animals raised on farms. The close picture-text matches support early readers in understanding the text. The text offers subtle challenges with compound and complex sentence structures. This book also introduces early readers to expository and content-specific vocabulary. The expository vocabulary is defined in the Words to Know section. Early readers may need assistance in reading some of these words. Readers also may need assistance in using the Table of Contents, Words to Know, Read More, Internet Sites and Index/Word List sections of the book.

Table of Contents

A farm is a place where people raise food. Some farmers grow crops. Other farmers raise animals. Some farmers do both.

Crops are plants that become food for people and animals. People eat food made from wheat, corn, and soybeans. Animals eat food made from alfalfa hay, soybeans, and corn.

Farmers use machines to plant crops. Tractors pull plows and planters. Plows break up the ground. Planters drop seeds into the ground.

Farmers also use machines to harvest crops. Harvest means to pick. Farmers harvest crops when the crops are ripe. A combine harvests crops like corn and soybeans.

Some farmers also raise animals. Farmers raise chickens to have eggs and meat. Farmers raise sheep to have meat and wool. People make sweaters and blankets out of wool.

Farmers raise cattle and pigs to have meat. Cattle are cows and bulls. Farmers raise dairy cows to have milk.

Farmers milk dairy cows in the morning and at night. The milk goes to factories. Workers use milk to make butter, cheese, and ice cream.

Farmers feed their animals every day. They keep the barns and pens clean. They take care of young animals.

Horses, dogs, and cats also live on farms. Horses and dogs help farmers move cattle and sheep from place to place. Cats catch mice that eat crops. Farmers also keep horses, dogs, and cats as pets.

Words to Know

alfalfa—a green plant with small leaves that is dried to make hay; people feed alfalfa hay to animals

butter—a yellow or white fat made from milk; people put butter on food or use it in cooking

cheese—a yellow or white food made from milk; people put cheese on bread or crackers or use it in cooking

combine—a machine that cuts down plants and takes out the seeds

corn—yellow or white seeds that grow on a tall, green plant; people and animals eat corn

crop—many plants grown together; people raise crops to use for food, to feed to animals, or to use in making other things

harvest—to pick or gather crops

plow—a machine that breaks up the ground

soybean—a seed that grows on a bushy plant; people use soybeans to make cooking oil, food, and ink

wheat—a seed that grows on a grasslike plant; people use wheat to make flour, bread, and other foods

wool—the thick, soft hair on sheep

22

Read More

Hill, Lee Sullivan. *Farms Feed the World.* Minneapolis: Carolrhoda Books, 1997

Kallen, Stuart A. *The Farm.* Field Trips. Minneapolis: Abdo & Daughters, 1997.

Ready, Dee. *Farmers.* Community Helpers. Mankato, Minn.: Bridgestone Books, 1997.

Internet Sites

Agriculture for Your Classroom
http://www.rescol.ca/collections/agriculture/home.html

Kids CORNer
http://www.ohiocorn.org/kids

Tours—#1 The Story of Milk
http://www.moomilk.com/tours/tour1-0.htm

Index/Word List

alfalfa hay, 7
animals, 5, 7, 13, 19
barns, 19
blankets, 13
bulls, 15
butter, 17
cats, 21
cattle, 15, 21
cheese, 17
chickens, 13
combine, 11
corn, 7, 11
cows, 15
crops, 5, 7, 9, 11, 21
dairy cows, 15, 17
dogs, 21

eggs, 13
factories, 17
farm, 5, 21
farmers, 5, 9, 11, 13,
    15, 17, 19, 21
food, 5, 7
ground, 9
horses, 21
ice cream, 17
machines, 9, 11
meat, 13, 15
mice, 21
milk, 15, 17
morning, 17
night, 17
pens, 19

people, 5, 7, 13
pets, 21
pigs, 15
place, 5
planters, 9
plants, 7
plows, 9
seeds, 9
sheep, 13, 21
soybeans, 7, 11
sweaters, 13
tractors, 9
wheat, 7
wool, 13

Word Count: **228**
Early-Intervention Level: **11**

Editorial Credits
Lois Wallentine, editor; James Franklin, design; Michelle L. Norstad, photo research

Capstone Press wishes to thank the National Farmers Union for reviewing the content
    of this book for accuracy.

Photo Credits
Dembinsky Photo Associates/Ron Goulet, cover; John Mielcarek, 1; Randall B. Henne, 10;
    Sharon Cummings, 12
Photo Network/Jeffry W. Myers, 14
Root Resources/Lia E. Munson, 4
Unicorn Stock Photos/Joel Dexter, 6; Ed Harp, 8; D&I MacDonald, 16; Alice M. Prescott, 18
Valan Photos/Phillip Norton, 20